P9-DMV-876

ANCIENT ROME
ACTIVITY BOOK

Author	Mary Jo Keller
Editor	Deneen Celecia
Assistant Editor	Linda Milliken
Designer	Wendy Loreen
Illustrator	Barb Lorseyedi

About the Author

Mary Jo Keller attended The College of New Rochelle in New Rochelle, New York and William and Mary in Williamsburg, Virginia. For the past thirteen years she has worked designing and implementing programs for various youth organizations such as the Boy Scouts of America and the Girl Scouts of America. She has also directed summer day camps for eight years.

Reproducible for classroom use only.
Not for use by an entire school or school system.

© 1995 **EDUPRESS** • P.O. Box 883 • Dana Point, CA 92629

ISBN 1-56472-032-2

M.Wablewski

Table Of Contents

Temple of Vesta — Rome

TEMPLES

ABOUT THE PHOTO

A Roman temple was believed to be the house of a god or goddess. The temple in the photograph was the "house" of Vesta, the goddess of the fireplace. Priestesses kept a fire burning constantly inside the temple. It was believed that Aeneas, the mythical founder of Rome, had brought the fire with him from the city of Troy. The shrine was carefully watched because it symbolized the safety of Rome.

Temples were built in the center of towns and cities for the important gods as well as gods considered special to the townspeople. Most temples were small with front porches supported by columns. The top of these columns were sculpted into beautiful designs.

ON YOUR OWN

You will need:
- White paper
- Pencil
- Drawing compass

Roman temples usually had two rows of columns in the front and a line of half columns along the sides. Using a compass to help you with circles or curves, draw your own design for the top of a column.

FUN WITH MORE THAN ONE

You will need:
- Paper
- Scissors
- Pencils
- Magazines
- Glue

Go on a column hunt with a partner! Make a list of all the different buildings you can think of that have columns either on the inside or outside. Make a collage using pictures cut from magazines of the buildings you have found.

TRIVIA TRACKDOWN

1. What is the name of the table located in a temple?

2. What is the name of the temple in Rome dedicated to all the gods?

3. What is this temple famous for?

4. What is the top part of a column called?

5. True or False? Some Roman temples were used to house great works of art, sculpture, state treasuries and the loot from wars.

6. What was kept in the *cella,* the locked room inside a temple?

1. Altar 2. The Pantheon 3. Its large dome 4. Capital 5. True 6. The statue of the god or goddess

Colosseum — Rome

COLOSSEUM

ABOUT THE PHOTO

The Colosseum is an example of the great skill of Roman architects and engineers. This huge amphitheater was built in 80 A.D. and was designed using arched vaults for strength.

A canvas awning would be stretched over the arena to provide shade. The Colosseum could even be lit at night by means of a giant chandelier suspended above the amphitheater. Beneath the arena lay a maze of cells and passages. There were elevators and trap doors that enabled men and animals to appear from beneath the floor. The arena could be flooded with water to stage a mock sea battle. Sadly, the "games" held in the arena resulted in the deaths of many men and animals.

ON YOUR OWN

You will need:
• Raw egg (Make sure there are no cracks)
• Basin

An egg is similar in shape to a three-dimensional arch like the ones found in the Colosseum. This is one of the strongest architectural forms and explains how the Colosseum could hold the weight of tons of concrete and 50,000 spectators! To show how strong this shape is, try to crush an egg in your hand. Take off any rings you may be wearing. Holding the egg over the basin, squeeze the egg in your palm as hard as you can. You won't be able to crush it, even using two hands!

FUN WITH MORE THAN ONE

You will need:
• Large sheet of white paper
• Crayons or colored pencils

Draw a large oval on a piece of paper. Inside the oval make a maze of corridors, rooms, elevator shafts and stairways. Make a start and finish. Trade your maze with another student. Enjoy solving each other's maze.

TRIVIA TRACKDOWN

1. What were the men called who fought in the Colosseum?

2. How was the outside of the Colosseum decorated?

3. What did a *bestiarius* fight against in the arena?

4. Name the word that means "theater on both sides".

5. What large piece of machinery was used to build the Colosseum and is still used today?

6. The name "Colosseum" comes from the colossal statue of which emperor that once stood on the arena's site?

1. Gladiators 2. With statues in each of the archways 3. Wild animals 4. Amphitheater 5. A crane 6. Nero

Ancient Rome Photo-Fun Activities © EDUPRESS

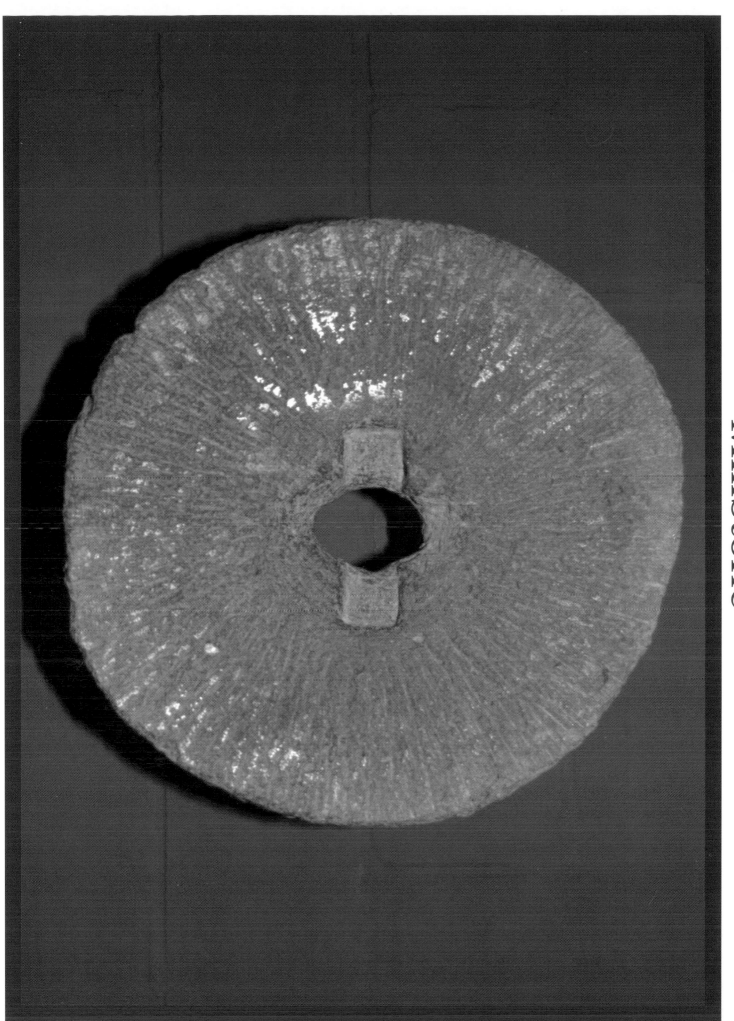

Millstone

MILLSTONE

ABOUT THE PHOTO

The large, round stone in the photograph is the upper stone from a set of two millstones used to grind grain into flour. The two indentations in the stone mark the spot where a wooden handle was once attached. The grain was shaken into the hole in the center of the upper stone. Slaves, mules or old horses pushed the handle so the upper stone turned. The grain was crushed between the roughened stones and emerged from the outer edges as flour!

Millstones were cut from the hardest material available. In Pompeii, archeologists discovered millstones cut from lava. The finest flour was milled when the stones had many grooves and were set close together.

ON YOUR OWN

You will need:
- Concrete surface, sidewalk or playground
- A stone about the size of your fist
- Assorted material to grind: popcorn kernels, rice, nuts, dried beans, cereal
- Dustpan and brush for clean up

To get an idea of what happens when a grain is stone-ground, try grinding several different food items from the list. Place the item on the cement and rub it for as long as it takes to grind it to a powder. You can see why this job was done by slaves or old horses! The millstone in the picture made this job easier. Study the diagram to see how the stone in the photo was used.

FUN WITH MORE THAN ONE

You will need:
- 2 envelopes fast-acting dry yeast
- 2½ cups (591.5 ml) tepid water
- 1 teaspoon (4.9 ml) salt
- Cornmeal
- 7 cups (1656.2 ml) bread flour
- ½ cup (118.3 ml) rye flour
- 1 cup (236.6 ml) whole wheat flour

Dissolve yeast in water in a large bowl. Add rye and wheat flour, salt and 1½ cups (354 ml) bread flour. Beat with electric mixer on high for ten minutes. Add remaining flour. Knead on a floured surface for ten minutes. Cover dough. Let rise until doubled. Punch down and let rise again. Punch down and form into two loaves. Place on cookie sheets dusted with cornmeal. Let rise. Bake at 450° F (229.9° C) for 25 minutes or until crust is gold.

TRIVIA TRACKDOWN

1. Who taught the Romans a lot about bread baking?

2. What is the word for "beating grain out of its husk"?

3. True or false? The Romans heated their bread ovens with natural gas.

4. Roman bread was made with dents on the top. Why?

5. What is yeast? Is it a tiny plant or a single-celled animal?

6. When you look at the stone in the picture, are you looking at its top or bottom surface?

1. The Greeks 2. Threshing 3. False, they used wood or charcoal 4. To make it easier to cut 5. Plant 6. You are looking at the bottom of the top stone

Memorial Marker

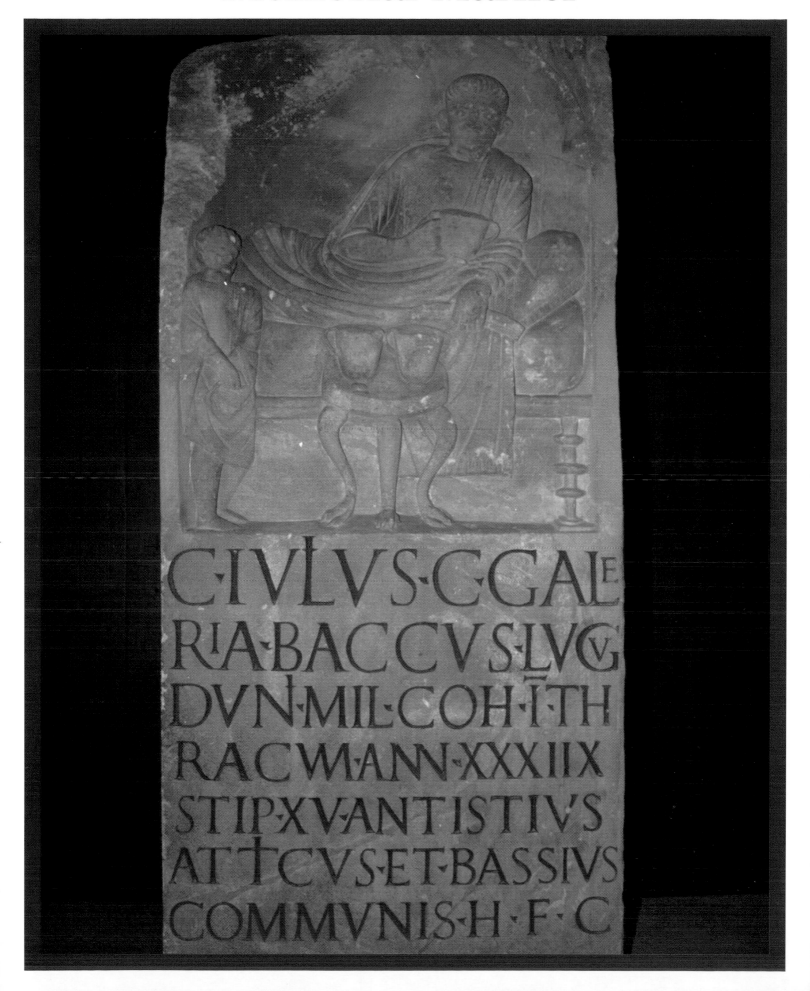

CIVLVS·C·GAL̄
RIA·BACCVS·LVḠ
DVN·MIL·COH·Ī·TH
RAC·M·ANN·XXXIIX
STIP·XV·ANTISTIVS
AT̄CVS·ET·BASSIVS
COMMVNIS·H·F·C

MEMORIAL

ABOUT THE PHOTO

Not even an expert stone-carver would begin cutting into the smooth stone of an important marker without careful planning! He had to consider the size of the stone, the number of words and each letter's width.

The man who inscribed the memorial stone in the photograph started his assignment by sketching his design on papyrus. When he was satisfied with his design, he marked straight lines on the stone. He did this by holding a chalk-coated string very tightly across the stone. He would pluck the string and let it snap back leaving a straight line of chalk dust behind. Only after tracing the letters onto the stone would he begin carving.

ON YOUR OWN

You will need:
- Paper
- Pencils

Write a story about the man on the memorial stone in the picture. Use the translations below to help you imagine what kind of life this man led in Ancient Rome! Share your stories with the class.

ATTICVS, BASSIVS—Men's names
STIPENDIUM—Military service
COMMVNIS—General
ANTISTITIS—High priest
CIVILVS—Citizen
LUGEO—To mourn
MILLE—1,000
XXXIIX—38
ET—And
XV—15

FUN WITH MORE THAN ONE

You will need:
- Large, rectangular piece of butcher paper
- String
- Black marking pens
- Ruler
- Colored chalk
- Pencils
- Drawing compass

Work with a partner to design a monument. Rub a long piece of string with chalk. Stretch the string tightly across the paper and snap it hard. Make several lines spaced about four inches (10 cm) apart. Use a ruler and compass to draw the letters. Post along the school's corridor. In ancient Rome, the roads were lined with memorials.

TRIVIA TRACKDOWN

1. What do we call a stone pillar that is set up on a road to show the distance between cities?

2. What is the name of the plant material used by Roman designers to write on?

3. True or False? Roman carvers used a drawing compass to help them arrange the letters on the stone they were to inscribe.

4. Did Roman stone carvers use upper or lower case letters in their inscriptions?

5. The Roman alphabet is based on another country's alphabet. Name this other country.

6. What is another name for a person who works with stone, brick or concrete?

1. Milestone 2. Papyrus 3. True 4. Upper case 5. Greece 6. Mason

Ancient Rome Photo-Fun Activities © EDUPRESS

Villa of Mysteries — Pompeii

VILLA OF MYSTERIES

ABOUT THE PHOTO

Much of our knowledge of daily life in Rome comes from the ruins of a city called Pompeii. When a volcano erupted in 79 A.D., it buried the city under layers of ashes which hardened and preserved the buildings. When the city was unearthed in the 18th century, countless wall fragments painted with flowers and scenes of people going about their daily lives were discovered.

These wall fragments came from the interior walls of homes and public buildings. Since wallpaper had not been invented yet, Roman home-owners often had beautiful paintings put directly onto the damp plaster of their walls. A painting on plaster is called a *fresco*.

ON YOUR OWN

You will need:
- Heavy cardboard carton
- Pencil
- Trimming knife
- Drywall mud
- Glue
- Ruler
- Tempera paint
- Paintbrushes

Cut two identical rectangles about 8 X 10 inches (10 X 25 cm) from the box. Draw a one inch (2.54 cm) border on one piece. Cut out the center. Glue the frame piece to the backing piece. Use a scrap of cardboard as a trowel to spread the pre-mixed plaster (drywall mud) inside the frame. Let plaster set until almost dry, but still damp. This will take three to five hours. Paint a picture directly onto the damp plaster. As the plaster dries, it sets the pigment.

FUN WITH MORE THAN ONE

You will need:
- Large sheets of white butcher paper
- Pencils
- Crayons

Cut a piece of butcher paper a foot (30 cm) or so longer than you are. Lie down on the paper and have your partner trace around you. Trace your partner's outline on a separate sheet. Have fun using crayons to add clothing and details to make it seem as if you were a part of a Roman wall mural.

TRIVIA TRACKDOWN

1. Name a word that means "a picture painted directly on a wall or ceiling".

2. Although most paintings were wall murals, some paintings were done on this material. Can you name it?

3. True or false? Still-life pictures of food and tableware were popular on Roman walls.

4. Is Pomeii located in Northern or Southern Italy?

5. What was the name of the volcano that erupted and buried Pompeii?

6. What do we call the study of ancient peoples and their cultures?

1. Mural 2. Wooden panels 3. True 4. Southern 5. Mount Vesuvius 6. Archaeology

Foot Soldier

FOOT SOLDIER

ABOUT THE PHOTO

The armor in the photograph was made from curved pieces of steel that went around a Roman soldier's chest, over his shoulders and was fastened together with leather straps. His helmet was hammered from sheet bronze and had side pieces to protect his face. Roman soldiers, or *legionaries,* carried a curved, oblong shield made by covering a wooden frame with leather and linen and bound with rawhide or hammered bronze. There was a *boss,* or raised part, in the middle with a handle behind.

Each infantryman carried two javelins and a sword hung on a leather strap over his left shoulder. A waist belt carried his sheath and dagger.

ON YOUR OWN

You will need:
- Paper plates
- Cardboard
- Gold spray-paint
- Long dowel, broom handle
- Permanent marker
- Aluminum foil
- Packing tape
- Scissors
- Paper
- Glue

A *signifer* carried the group's standard or emblem, called the signum. Make one by covering three paper plates with foil. Cut out the center of another paper plate. Cut leaf shapes from scraps and glue to the circle to make a wreath. Cut a narrow rectangle from cardboard. Paint the wreath and nameplate gold. Write your group's name on the nameplate. Attach the wreath, nameplate and silver plates to the staff. Add paper streamers.

GREENS

FUN WITH MORE THAN ONE

You will need:
- Playground or field
- Heavy cardboard pieces, about 2 X 3 feet (90 cm)
- Trimming knife
- At least nine "soldiers"

Roman soldiers could cover themselves with their shields to make a *testudo,* or tortoise. Make a shield by cuting two slits in the center of the cardboard to make a handle. Shield corners line up in even rows— a minimum of three rows of three. The center row(s) holds their shields over their heads. The outside rows hold their shields to the sides. Practice walking in formation.

TRIVIA TRACKDOWN

1. What type of armor worn by early Roman soldiers was made of tiny iron rings connected together by wire?

2. True or false? A soldier wore a scarf to keep his armor from rubbing his neck.

3. A javelin is a type of _____?

4. What machine was used to throw huge rocks at the enemy?

5. Archers shot behind a protective screen made from wickerwork and covered with what?

6. How many soldiers made up a century in early Roman armies?

1. Mail 2. True 3. Spear 4. Catapult 5. Animal hides 6. 100

ROMAN STATUES

ABOUT THE PHOTO

Busts like the one in the photograph were very popular in classical Rome. Statues of emperors, gods, goddesses and famous people could be found in temples, public buildings and even in the streets! Statues ranged in size from miniature statuettes to colossal figures and were often painted. Wealthy Romans had statues or busts of their ancestors made for display within their own homes.

These portrait sculptures tell us a lot about what the Roman people looked like and how they dressed. Roman men favored short hair combed forward and close-cropped beards. A hooked nose was considered attractive. Women wore elaborate hairstyles and jewelry.

ON YOUR OWN

You will need:
- White construction paper or drawing paper
- Crayons or colored pencils
- Pencil

Draw a picture of yourself as you might have appeared to a Roman sculptor if a statue was made of you. Make sure you are wearing a toga and your hair is arranged in the Roman style. Because marble statues were often painted, color your drawing with crayons or colored pencils.

FUN WITH MORE THAN ONE

You will need:
- Playground

Play a game of statues with your classmates. One person is chosen to be "it". This person covers their eyes and silently counts to ten. Meanwhile, everyone moves around until the person who is "it" calls, "FREEZE!" Everyone is turned into statues in a Roman villa! The first person who moves becomes "it".

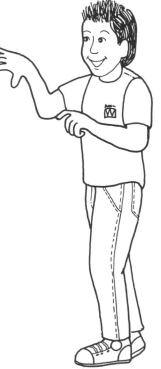

TRIVIA TRACKDOWN

1. Many statues in Rome were imported from what country?

2. Name another material used by Roman sculptors.

3. True or false? Roman artists could create a stone head that looked very realistic.

4. What word means "a piece of sculpture representing the head and shoulders of a human body"?

5. In Washington D.C., there is a giant statue of a famous U.S. president. Can you name him?

6. What is the name of the sharp-edged tool used to shape stone?

1. Greece 2. Bronze 3. True 4. Bust 5. Abraham Lincoln 6. Chisel

Sculptured Bust

Pottery Jars (Amphorae)

AMPHORAE

ABOUT THE PHOTO

An *amphora* is a two-handled, earthenware jar used to hold grain, wine, olive oil or fish sauce. The photograph does not show the pointed bottoms of the amphorae. Some of these jars were so large they had to be carried by two men who would hang the jug from a strong stick. They would walk single file with the stick resting on their shoulders and the jug suspended between them.

The long narrow shape of these jars allowed them to be thrust into the earth, stored upright in rocks or packed together in the holds of merchant ships. Some ships could carry as many as 6,000 amphorae because their unusual shape made them nest together very efficiently.

ON YOUR OWN

You will need:
• Paper   • Pencil   • Thesaurus

An amphora is a kind of jar. A synonym is a word that has the same meaning as another word. A thesaurus is a book of synonyms. List as many synonyms for the word amphora or jar as you can. Check the thesaurus to see how you did!

FUN WITH MORE THAN ONE

You will need:
• Playground or field
• Strong stick or dowel about five feet long
• Bucket   • Rope or twine   • Water

Pretend you and a friend are Roman merchant seamen carrying an amphora filled with olive oil to the ship. Slide the stick through the handle of the bucket and secure with the rope. Fill the bucket partway with water. Practice lifting and carrying the "amphora" without sloshing any water!

TRIVIA TRACKDOWN

1. Romans imported more than 40,000 tons of what product grown in Africa and Egypt?

2. Beacause this oil soaks into the pottery, jars that held it were destroyed and used for ship's ballast. Name the oil.

3. True or False? Roman merchant seamen used compasses to help them navigate.

4. Were goods usually transported by land or by sea?

5. Ostia was an important port because it was connected to Rome by a river. Name the river.

6. True or false? *Amphoras* is the plural of the word *amphora*.

1. Grain 2. Olive oil 3. False 4. Sea 5. Tiber River 6. False, the plural of amphora is amphorae because it is a Latin word.

Literature List

• *City: A Story of
   Roman Planning and Construction*
by David Macaulay;
Houghton Mifflin 1974. (3-6)
The planning and construction of an
imaginary Roman city is set forth in clear
pen-and-ink illustrations and a lucid text.

• *Daughter of Earth: A Roman Myth*
by Gerald McDermott;
Delacorte 1984. (2-4)
A retelling of the myth of Ceres, the earth
mother, and her daughter Proserpina.

• *Romans*
by Nicola Baxter;
Watts LB 1992. (3-6)
Crafts and projects such as creating a
mosaic and building a Roman villa.

• *Classical Rome*
by John D. Clare;
Harcourt 1993. (3-6)
This introduction to ancient Rome shows
photos of people in period costume with
informative text.

• *Science in Ancient Rome*
by Jacqueline L. Harris;
Watts LB 1988. (5-7)
A description of Roman achievements in
applied science.

• *The Secrets of Vesuvius:
   Exploring the Mysteries of an
   Ancient Buried City*
by Sara C. Bisel; Scholastic 1991. (4-7)
A physical anthropologist describes the
Roman city of Herculaneum which was
destroyed by the eruption of Vesuvius.

• *The Romans*
by Pamela Odijk;
Silver LB 1989. (4-7)
An oversize book about the ancient
Romans and their way of life.

• *Roman Forts*
by Margaret Mulvihill;
Watts LB 1990. (4-6)
Describes Roman forts, the weapons used
and the life led by soldiers of the period.

• *Pompeii*
by Timothy Biel;
Lucent Books LB 1989. (4-6)
This book covers the history of the city of
Pompeii and tells how the residents lived
prior to the eruption of Mount Vesuvius.

• *Heroes, Gods and Emperors
   from Roman Mythology*
by Kerry Usher;
Bedrick 1992. (5-7)
The story of the *Aeneid* plus those of the
Tarquino and Romulus and Remus are
three of the legends retold.

• *The Assassination of Julius Caesar*
by George Ochoa; Silver LB 1991. (5-7)
The events that led to the assassination of
Julius Caesar in Rome.

• *A Roman Villa*
by Jacqueline Morley;
Bedrick LB 1992. (4-6)
Through many double-page spreads and
cutaway drawings, the interiors and
exteriors of Roman villas are explored.

Roman Empire

Historical Aid

Ancient Rome began as a small community of shepherds in Northern Italy and grew to become one of the greatest empires in history.

Perhaps the greatest accomplishment of the empire was the *Pax Romana* (Roman Peace). For the first time, the entire Mediterranean area was at peace and under one government.

Trade and prosperity thrived. The Roman navy had suppressed the pirates so merchant ships could sail safely. A vast network of roads made trade and travel with the provinces possible.

Project

Compare the Ancient Roman Empire map with the current geographic area.

Materials

- Ancient Roman Empire map, following
- Current world map
- Pencils
- Paper

Directions

1. Make a copy of the map of the Roman empire for each student or group of students. Make sure everyone has access to a current world map.

2. On a separate sheet of paper, have students make a list of the modern countries that were once part of the ancient Roman empire.

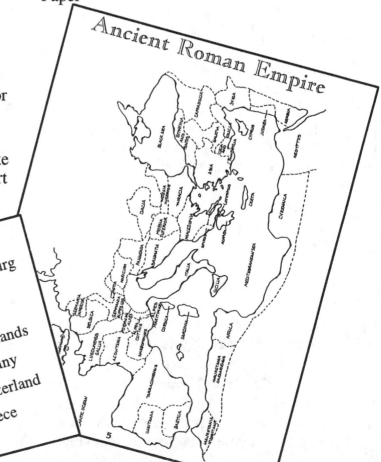

Italy
France
Spain
Luxembourg
Egypt
Belgium
England
The Netherlands
Wales
Germany
Portugal
Switzerland
Andorra
Greece
Romania

© EDUPRESS

Ancient Roman Empire

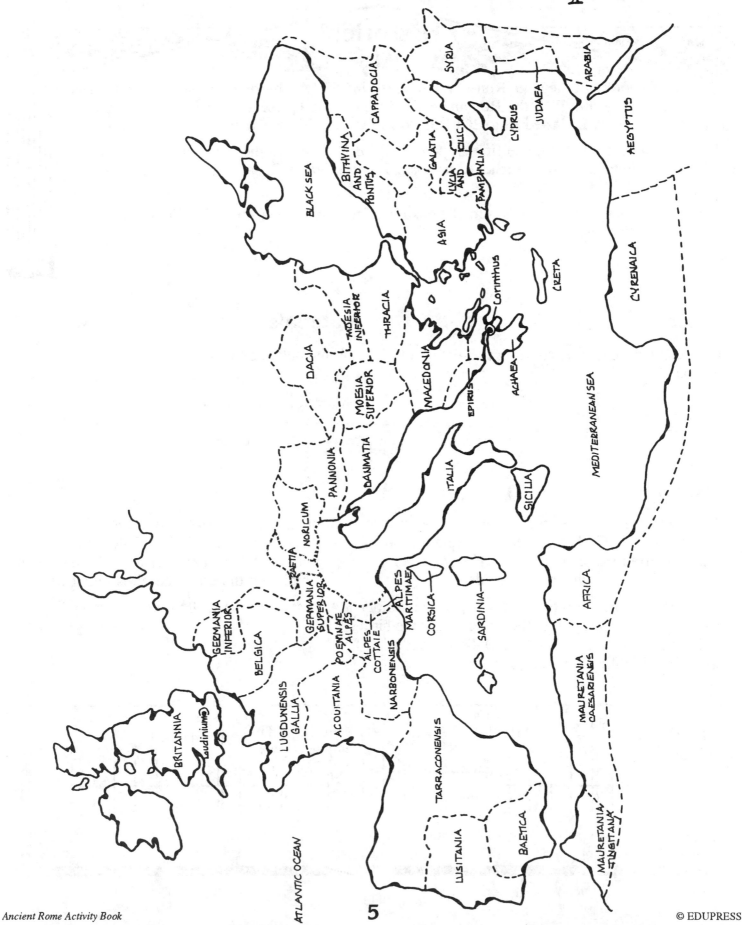

Time Line

Historical Aid

According to legend, Rome was founded in 753 B.C. by twin brothers Romulus and Remus. By 509 B.C. the Romans had driven out the Etruscans and formed a republic. The Punic Wars lasted from 264 B.C. to 146 B.C. as Rome expanded overseas.

Augustus became the first emperor in 27 B.C. Between the years of 96 A.D. to 180 A.D. the Roman empire reached its peak. The year 395 A.D. saw the vast Roman empire split into two parts.

The last emperor, Romulus Augustulus, was overthrown in 476 A.D., marking the end of the empire.

Project

Learn about a time line by charting the history of the Roman empire.

Materials

- White butcher paper
- Rulers
- Marking pens or crayons

Directions

1. Define the terms A.D. (Anno Domini-in the year of the Lord) and B.C. (before Christ). Explain how dates are arranged on a time line. The years before Christ (B.C.) are counted backwards.

2. Stretch out a long sheet of butcher paper on the floor and draw a long line across the paper. Mark the birth of Christ in the center (1 A.D.). Make 15 marks in each direction. Each mark represents 50 years.

3. Instruct the students to use the information in the the Historical Aid to place the most important dates in the history of the Roman Empire on the time line. Illustrate if desired.

4. Post on a long wall in the classroom.

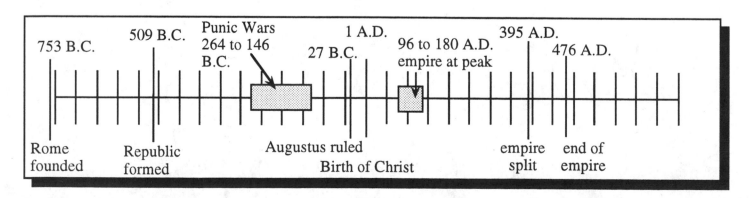

Roman Law

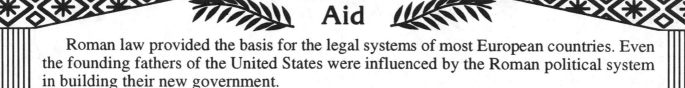

Historical Aid

Roman law provided the basis for the legal systems of most European countries. Even the founding fathers of the United States were influenced by the Roman political system in building their new government.

The Romans published their first code of law, The Laws of the Twelve Tables, during the early days of the Republic. These early laws primarily dealt with the family and family property.

Through the years, a general set of laws developed for all the people under Roman rule. Lawyers called these laws the *Jus Gentium*, or Law of Nations. These rules were based on common sense notions of fairness.

Project

Have the students develop a list of classroom "laws".

Materials

• White butcher paper
• Marking pens

Directions

1. Have the students discuss what they feel should be classroom rules that are fair for everyone, including teachers.

2. List these rules on the butcher paper.

3. Post the rules for everyone to read.

Jus Gentium

1. No yelling in the classroom.

2. Ask permission before leaving the classroom.

3. No name calling.

Government

Historical Aid

During the early years of the Roman period, people were ruled by a king. But in 509 B.C. nobles threw out the wicked king and formed a republic. All the free citizens of the republic had a vote.

Two consuls who acted as heads of state and controlled the armed forces were elected each year. Other government officials included *Quaestors* who dealt with the finances, *Censors* who kept a register of citizens's names, *Tribunes* who protected the interests of working people and *Aediles* who supervised public works.

Project

Design campaign posters for a classroom election.

Materials

- White paper
- Colored markers or crayons

Directions

1. On a piece of white paper, draw and color campaign posters. Have the students imagine they are running for class Consul (president), Censor (roll-keeper), Quaestor (treasurer), Tribune (speaker for students' rights), or Aedile (maintenance supervisor).

2. Display the posters by hanging them on the classroom walls. In Roman times, the posters would have been painted directly onto the walls of the city.

3. Have an actual election to fill these positions.

SAM
for
CLASS CONSUL

Great Leader
for a
Great Class

Newspaper

Historical Aid

In the Roman capital, news was spread by means of a newssheet called *Acta Diurna* or Daily Events. The paper reported on the new laws and important events.

Since there weren't any printing presses, the newssheet had to be copied by hand. The papers were posted throughout the city so people could gather and read the latest news.

Project

Publish a classroom issue of the Acta Diurna (Daily Events).

Materials

- Paper
- Pen

Directions

1. Have the students write short news stories on the happenings in their classroom. This might include a list of classroom rules, upcoming school events as well as an item about their Roman studies.

2. Compile the articles under the heading: **Acta Diurna**. Make several copies and post around the school.

Postal System

The Roman government developed a highly organized postal system to keep in contact with its far-flung outposts. The straight, smooth roads designed by the engineers were superior to all other roads of the time and made the efficient delivery of mail possible.

Mail was delivered by way of a relay system established by Augustus Caesar. Mounted couriers rode throughout the empire stopping at relay stations called posthouses. There, messengers could rest, pass the mail on to another courier or get a fresh horse. At first, only government mail could be delivered by the couriers.

Project

Learn about how the Roman relay system works by having a relay race.

Materials

• One envelope per team
• Masking tape or cones to mark the finish line

Directions

1. Divide students into teams of four. Mark the start and finish lines. Evenly space the team members along the course.

2. Give the first member on each team an envelope. On the START signal have them run to the next team member and pass on the envelope. The first team who delivers the mail over the finish line is the winner.

3. Race in heats, if necessary, to give everyone a chance to run.

Cities

Historical Aid

Cities in the Roman Empire served as centers of trade and culture. Many cities began as army camps and, therefore, had an orderly layout. The engineers that did the planning were careful to include water supplies and sewer systems as well as sport arenas, theaters, baths and a forum.

The forum was a large open space surrounded by markets, temples and government buildings. The first forum was built in the city of Rome and was called the Forum Romanum.

Project

Cooperative teams of students work as city planners.

Materials

- White butcher paper
- Pencils
- Marking pens
- Rulers
- Chalkboard
- Chalk

Directions

1. Have the students brainstorm on the various facilities and services a city needs to function efficiently. List these ideas on the chalkboard.

2. Divide the class into teams of four. Give each team a large sheet of white butcher paper.

3. Allow the teams sufficient time to design and draw a plan for their city. As each team shares their plan, have them explain how their city meets the needs on the list.

 © EDUPRESS

Architecture

Historical Aid

The Romans were great builders. In addition to houses, temples and palaces, the Romans constructed aqueducts to carry water to cities, giant outdoor arenas, shops, theaters and baths.

Roman engineers invented two forms of roof design, the arch and the dome. Concrete as a building material was developed by the Romans.

The Pantheon is an ancient temple that still stands in the center of Rome. Built of fired brick and concrete it has a domed roof that rises 142 feet (43 meters) above the floor! Many of the engineering techniques used to build the Pantheon are still in use today.

Project

Learn about arches by making a paper replica to edge a classroom doorway.

Materials

- Light gray butcher paper or white butcher paper painted gray
- Gray and black tempera paint
- Large sponges
- Scissors
- Shallow pans such as aluminum pie tins to hold paint
- Newspaper
- Paintbrushes
- Tape
- Black marking pen

Directions

1. Spread out newspaper on floor or parking lot. Lay out three long sheets of butcher paper or enough to edge the classroom door.

2. Dip sponges into gray paint and lightly press onto paper to achieve a concrete appearance. Using a paintbrush dipped into black paint, spatter the paper with black dots to look like the bits of volcanic material that were an ingredient in Roman cement.

3. Tape the sheets together to form a border for the doorway. Draw an arch with the marking pen. Outline the stones. Take special care when outlining the keystone at the top of the arch—it holds the other stones in place!

4. Cut out and tape to the wall.

Weights & Measures

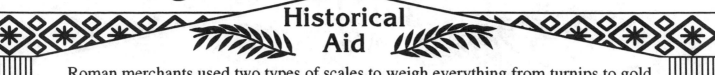

Historical Aid

Roman merchants used two types of scales to weigh everything from turnips to gold. A balance scale is simply a horizontal beam with a pan suspended on each end. The object being weighed is placed in one pan. Weights of known quantities are placed in the other pan until the two pans balance. The steelyard was developed by the Romans. The scale used in a physician's office is a type of steelyard still used today!

To keep merchants from cheating their customers with false measures, the weights they used were checked by various officials. Standard weights and measures were established to be used throughout the empire.

Project

Compare the weights and measures the Romans used with today's measures.

Directions

Divide students into teams. Using the measuring tools and supplies have them find the answers to the following questions:

1. What is your height in "Roman feet"?
2. How many cups in a sextarius?
3. Is a liter of water of water more or less than a sextarius?
4. How many libra in 1 ½ pounds?
5. How long is one of your paces? How many of your paces are in a mille passuum?

Materials

- Scale that measures ounces like a postal scale
- Ruler
- Cup measure
- Bowls
- Water
- Dried beans
- Measuring tape
- Liter bottle
- Cups

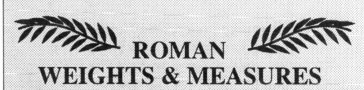

ROMAN WEIGHTS & MEASURES

Sextarius = a measure for liquid and corn that equals approximately ½ quart

Pes = a Roman foot, approximately 11 ⅔"

Libra = a measure of weight that equals 11 ½ ounces

Mille passuum = a Roman mile, approximately 9/10 of a mile. Literally translated as "one thousand paces".

Coins

Historical Aid

The Romans had no proper coinage until the 3rd century B.C. Until then, the value of things was worked out in terms of livestock.

Coins were minted by the emperor mainly to pay the soldiers wages and to collect taxes. Almost everyone across the empire used the same coinage, which made the trading business much simpler.

The Emperors issued coins that featured their own portrait on the obverse side. Coins were a good way to show people the image of the emperor and his deeds since there were no televisions or newspapers.

Project

The students can design a coin using themselves as the model.

Materials

- Paper
- Round circle template or protractor
- Pencil or thin marking pen
- Crayons or markers

Directions

1. Instruct the students to pretend they are a new emperor preparing to issue his coin. Have them draw two circles on the paper, one for the obverse side and the other for the reverse side.

2. The students can draw their coins featuring their own portrait and title on one side and their own design on the reverse side.

Numerals

The Romans created a system of number symbols that made it possible to write all the numbers from 1 to 1,000,000 with only seven symbols. Arithmetic, however, is very difficult to do using Roman numerals. Unlike the Arabic numbers we use today, Roman numerals were written as strings of symbols to be added together. This made large numbers very long and complicated. For example, the number 948 would be written as DCCCCXXXXVIII.

The early Roman numeral system differed from the system we're familiar with. Early Romans used IIII instead of IV for four, VIIII instead of IX for nine, ↓ instead of L for fifty and CIƆ instead of M for one thousand.

Project

Practice writing Roman numerals.

Materials

- Paper
- Pencil

Directions

1. Copy the number chart onto the chalkboard.

2. Have the students try to write out their phone number, date and address.

3. For an added challenge, have them try a few simple arithmatic problems.

Roman Numerals About 500 B.C.

I	one
II	two
III	three
IIII	four
V	five
VI	six
VII	seven
VIII	eight
VIIII	nine
X	ten
↓	fifty
C	one hundred
D	five hundred
CIƆ	one thousand

Calendar

At first, the Roman calendar had only 304 days divided into ten months. The months were called Martius, Aprilis, Maius, Junius, Quintilis, Sextilis, September, October, November and December. The Roman ruler Numa added Januarius and Februarius, but the calendar was still not correct because winter didn't always arrive in December! Julius Caesar ordered the astronomer Sosigenes to set things right. This Julian calendar was widely used for 1,500 years.

Quintilis and Sextilis were renamed Julius and Augustus to honor Julius Caesar and Augustus Caesar. Augustus added one extra day to his month to make sure he had as many days in his month as Julius Caesar had in his.

Project

Make a classroom calendar using the Roman names for the months.

Materials

- Marking pens or crayons
- Paper
- Ruler
- Pencil
- Stapler

Directions

1. Give each group of twelve students a piece of paper. Instruct them to use the ruler and pencil to mark off five rows of seven squared columns.

2. Have the students label the month and days of the week. Have them fill in the year and the dates.

3. Decorate the calendar with markers or crayons. Staple the pages together and display.

Roman Names of the Months

Januarius	Julius
Februarius	Augustus
Martius	September
Aprilis	October
Maius	November
Junius	December

Home Life

Historical Aid

In the cities, most Romans lived in crowded apartment buildings, but the wealthy could afford houses. These elegant homes were built around a spacious courtyard called an atrium. The atrium had a large roof opening and the rain was caught in a pool that drained under the stone floor.

The rooms surrounding the courtyard had high ceilings and wide doorways, but few windows. The walls were brightly painted and the floors were often decorated with mosaics. There was little furniture to clutter the rooms.

Large houses also had a colonnaded garden called a *parastyle* at the back, laid out with statues, shrubs, flower beds and herbs for the kitchen.

Project

Build a diorama of a Roman courtyard.

Directions

1. Paint the shoebox inside and out with a bright color.

2. Set the box upright. Cut door openings in all four sides of the box.

3. Cut a piece of construction paper to fit the floor of the box. Glue a rectangle of aluminum foil to the center to make the pool. Using markers or crayons, design a pattern on the floor to simulate marble tiles. Glue the floor in place.

4. On a separate sheet of white paper use crayons, markers or paint to make wall murals. Glue onto "walls" of the box. Make columns by drawing vertical lines on paper, roll paper around pencil and tape. Glue to edge doorways.

5. Make a household shrine (see page 18). On paper draw a shrine with a sculpture or picture of an ancestor in it and cut out. Cut small squares from cardboard and glue several together to hold the shrine away from the wall. Glue the shrine cutout to the cardboard, trimming away excess. Glue to wall.

6. Add figures cut from paper and a bench made from cardboard.

Materials

- Shoebox
- Scissors
- Tempera paints, crayons or markers
- Construction paper
- White paper
- Aluminum foil
- Tape
- Glue
- Paintbrushes
- Cardboard (the box lid would work well)

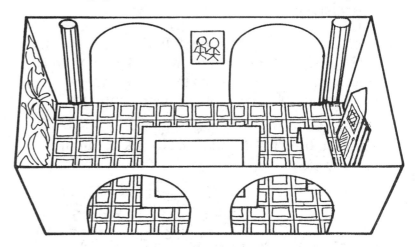

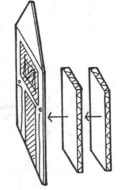

Household Gods

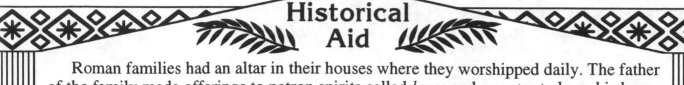

Historical Aid

Roman families had an altar in their houses where they worshipped daily. The father of the family made offerings to patron spirits called *lares* and *panates* to keep his home and family safe.

The *lar* was a spirit of a family's ancestor. Most Romans felt it was very important to remember their forefather. Senatorial families kept wax masks or portraits of their ancestors. People would visit the tombs of their ancestors frequently as a way of honoring their memories.

Project

Learning about one's grandparents or great-grandparents is a good way to honor them.

Materials

- Photographs from home
- "My Family's History" page, following
- Family momentos (optional)

Directions

1. Reproduce one copy of the "My Family's History" sheet for each student to take home and fill in. Remind the students they may bring in photographs or a memento of their family to share.

2. Set aside time for the students to talk about their ancestry.

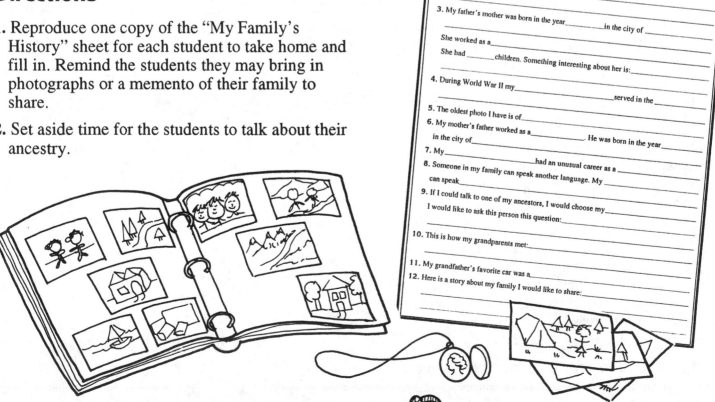

My Family's History

1. My father's grandfather's name was_____
2. My grandmothers' maiden names were_____ and_____
3. My father's mother was born in the year_____ in the city of_____
   _____
   She worked as a_____
   She had _____ children. Something interesting about her is:_____
   _____
4. During World War II my_____
   _____ served in the_____
5. The oldest photo I have is of_____
6. My mother's father worked as a_____. He was born in the year_____
   in the city of_____
7. My_____ had an unusual career as a_____
8. Someone in my family can speak another language. My_____ can speak_____
9. If I could talk to one of my ancestors, I would choose my_____
   I would like to ask this person this question:_____
10. This is how my grandparents met:_____
    _____
11. My grandfather's favorite car was a_____
12. Here is a story about my family I would like to share:_____
    _____

My Family's History

1. My father's grandfather's name was_____

2. My grandmothers' maiden names were_____

   and_____

3. My father's mother was born in the year_____in the city of _____

   _____

   She worked as a_____

   She had _____children. Something interesting about her is:_____

   _____

4. During World War II my_____served in the _____

   _____

5. The oldest photo I have is of_____

6. My mother's father worked as a_____. He was born in the year_____

   in the city of_____

7. My_____had an unusual career as a _____

8. Someone in my family can speak another language. My _____

   can speak_____

9. If I could talk to one of my ancestors, I would choose my_____

   I would like to ask this person this question:_____

   _____

10. This is how my grandparents met:_____

    _____

11. My grandfather's favorite car was a_____

12. Here is a story about my family I would like to share:_____

    _____

    _____

Mythology

Historical Aid

The Romans believed in the existence of many different gods and spirits. Everyone was expected to make offerings and sacrifices to the gods. Because the Romans believed the gods controlled everything they did, it was important to try to make them friendly. Roman gods and goddesses were depicted in human forms, but larger and more powerful. Many Roman gods were taken from the Greeks and given new names.

Project

Write a resume for a god or goddess.

Materials

- Paper
- Pencils
- Information page about gods and goddesses, following

Directions

1. Have the students imagine they are helping a god or goddess find a job.

2. Decide if you wish to have the students do research on their own or use the information page.

3. Instruct them to summarize their god's past job experiences, strengths and talents, family history and anything special about them that an employer would find interesting.

  © EDUPRESS

Gods and Goddesses

GODS

MERCURY—messenger of the gods and the god of commerce, science and protector of travelers. Mercury was portrayed as a crafty, handsome young man wearing winged sandals, hat and carrying a winged staff.

MARS—the god of war and father of Romulus and Remus, the legendary founders of Rome. He is portrayed as wearing armor and a crested helmet. The wolf and the woodpecker are associated with Mars.

CUPID—the god of love is portrayed as a chubby infant with wings and holding a bow and arrow. A person shot with one of Cupid's arrows supposedly fell in love.

JUPITER—king of the gods and ruler of the universe. He was the father of Vulcan and Mars, among others. He was the god of weather and used a thunderbolt as a weapon.

NEPTUNE—god of the sea. He could cause or prevent storms at sea. He was also the god of earthquakes and horses. Neptune was often shown carrying a trident (three-headed spear) or riding on a chariot pulled by sea horses and accompanied by dolphins.

APOLLO—the god of light and the sun. He wrote poetry and played the lyre. He also had healing powers and could tell the future. Artists portrayed him as a handsome young man.

VULCAN—the god of fire. He worked as the blacksmith of the gods and was also the god of metalworking.

GODDESSES

MINERVA—one of the most important goddesses. She was the favorite of Jupiter and was the goddess of war and wisdom. She was depicted as a beautiful woman wearing armor and a helmet and carrying a magic shield. She also represented skill and handicrafts. The owl has traditionally been considered wise because it was Minerva's bird.

DIANA—goddess of the moon, hunting and all living things, especially young animals. Artists showed her wearing hunting clothes and carrying a bow and quiver of arrows accompanied by hunting dogs.

VESTA—goddess of the hearth. She was worshiped by Roman families as a household deity. She had a round temple dedicated to her in Rome in which a fire was always kept burning.

Clothing

Roman men, women and children wore a loose fitting garment called a *tunic*. Soldiers wore their tunics short, but a woman wore hers to ankle length. Only men who were Roman citizens could wear a *toga* over their tunic. A toga was a semicircular piece of white cloth about 18 feet long that draped around the entire body. A purple border edged the togas of the upper class only!

Women wore a dress called a *stola* over their tunics. These garments were made of linen, wool or silk dyed a variety of rich colors. When going outdoors, a Roman woman would drape herself in a very large shawl called a *palla*.

Project

Practice draping a toga as a Roman citizen would have done centuries ago.

Materials

- White paper tablecloth that comes on a roll, available at restaurant supply or party stores (approximately 15' per student) *or* white sheets that can be cut

Directions

1. Cut the sheet or tablecloth into lengths three times the height of the student. This was how Roman citizens were measured for their togas.

2. Cut the fabric into a semi-circle. Drape one end of the material over the left shoulder from back to front. Pass the other end under the right arm and across the left shoulder.

Wigs & Makeup

Historical Aid

Many Roman women used makeup. To achieve a fashionably pale complexion a woman would dust her face with powdered chalk or even white lead. (Many cosmetics were poisonous.) Cheeks and lips were stained with red ocher.

Elaborate hairstyles became quite popular at one time. Hairpieces and wigs were often used to achieve the desired look. Hair for wigs came from dark-haired Indian girls or blonde German girls who were captured in a military campaign. It was fashionable for men to wear their hair combed forward.

Project

Make a hairpiece similar to one worn by a Roman matron.

Materials

- Brown, yellow or black construction paper
- Brown, yellow or black yarn
- Scissors
- Glue
- Stapler
- Bobby pins

Directions

1. Fold over the two corners on the long edge of the construction paper and staple together.

2. Working in pairs, have one student hold the lengths of yarn while his partner braids them into plaits.

3. Glue the braids onto the construction paper, making loops or rows or circles.

4. Hold the wig in place with bobby pins.

5. (Optional) Boys may bring their own combs from home to comb their hair forward.

Jewelry

Historical Aid

Rings and bracelets were worn by both Roman men and women. Gold bracelets were awarded to soldiers who were brave in battle. The wearing of rings was regulated by law. Only freeborn citizens were allowed to wear gold rings. Some rings with carved stones were used to seal documents.

The Romans were probably the first to use rings as a symbol of engagement. A wedding ring sometimes had a tiny key attached to it as a symbol of the wife's authority in the household. Women also wore necklaces and earrings made of gold and precious stones.

Project

Make several pieces of Roman style jewelry.

Directions

Read and follow the directions for the projects on this and the following page.

Materials

- Aluminum foil
- Gold spray-paint
- Chenille sticks
- Scissors
- Glue
- White and colored plastic lids from coffee, oatmeal or nut cans
- Pencils
- Buttons with two holes
- Tagboard
- Magazine pages
- String
- Hot glue gun
- Pennies
- Stapler
- Black marker
- Pin backs

SNAKE ARMBAND

1. Cut a piece of aluminum foil about 8" (20.32 cm) long. Lay a chenille stick on the foil longways and fold it over and over to make a foil strip about 1" (2.54 cm) wide.

2. Cut two snakeheads from tagboard and cover with foil. Glue and staple to ends of foil strip. Spray-paint gold if you wish. Using a black permanent marker, gently draw on the snake's eyes and scales.

3. Coil around the arm.

Jewelry

NECKLACE
Make a necklace using gold and beads, a popular combination in Roman jewelry.

1. Cut magazine pages into long thin triangles the length of the page.
2. Roll up from the wide end around a straw. Glue the point in place.
3. Spray-paint some beads gold.
4. Thread on string to make a necklace.

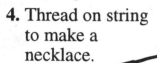

CUFF BRACELET
Make a bracelet like the ones given to Roman soldiers.

1. Cut tagboard to fit wrist for a bracelet. Cover with aluminum foil and spray-paint gold.
2. With a permanant marker, copy S•P•Q•R on the bracelet. This stands for Senatus Populus que Romanus (The Senate and the Roman People). This symbol of Rome was used in art, writing and architecture.
3. Staple ends together.

CAMEO BROOCH
Make a cameo brooch similar to one worn by a Roman woman on her gown.

1. Cut an oval from colored plastic lid. Cut a larger oval from tagboard. Cover tagboard oval with aluminum foil and spray-paint gold.
2. Trace outline of profile on white plastic lid. Cut out and glue to colored plastic oval. Glue to foil-covered oval.
3. Glue pin back to back of oval.

RINGS
Rings made from coins were a popular design among the Romans.

1. Use a button with two holes. Push a chenille stick up through one hole and back down into the other. Twist the ends of the stick together, adjusting to fit.
2. Use a glue gun to attach a penny to the button.

Education

Historical Aid

There were no public schools in ancient Rome so many children were taught at home. Some students attended private school. In either case, a child's education usually ended around age eleven.

A young man who was planning on becoming a lawyer or politician would study rhetoric or the art of public speaking and persuasion. This training helped him develop the skills needed to argue cases in a court of law or debate issues in the Senate.

Women were not allowed to become lawyers or politicians. In fact, most girls received no formal education at all.

Project

Have the students form debate teams to practice the art of rhetoric and the concepts of pro and con.

Materials

- Butcher paper
- Markers
- Pencils
- Paper

Directions

1. Brainstorm some debate topics or choose from the sample topics. Each topic needs two teams—one pro and one con. Define the words debate, pro and con and rebuttal.

2. Divide the class into teams of four to six students and have them choose a speaker. Give each team five to ten minutes to prepare their argument. Their statements should be two minutes long.

3. Arrange desks so the teams face the class. Open with the pro side giving their statement. Use a timer if you wish. Give the con team the same amount of time to make their statement.

4. Each team gets an additional three minutes to respond to the other team's statement.

5. Conclude with a class vote of a show of hands for the most convincing team.

SAMPLE TOPICS

Should teachers give homework?

Should uniforms be required to wear at school?

Should the cafeteria serve breakfast as well as lunch?

Should there be candy and soda machines for the students to use?

Feast

Historical Aid

Wealthy Romans ate their large meal of the day in the midafternoon. They usually feasted for hours. Since the oil lamps gave off such little light, most Romans finished dinner before sunset and went to bed when it got dark.

A Roman feast would consist of many courses and entertainment as well. Guests would be invited and everyone would eat while reclining on large couches arranged around low tables. The meal was eaten with the fingers. The only tableware used was the spoon. Diners frequently washed their hands during dinner!

Project

Try eating while lying down!

Directions

1. Wash fruit and vegetables and arrange on trays with other food.

2. Push aside desks and spread out beach towels to cover floor.

3. Have the students lie down and put out food trays and water bowls for washing their hands.

4. Ask students if they got comfortable by lying on the floor. Remind them that many Roman couches were hard benches and not upholstered.

Materials

- Dates stuffed with nuts
- Various fruit such as apples, figs, cherries, peaches, grapes, pears and plums
- Various vegetables such as peas, parsnips, turnips, green beans, radishes, celery, lettuce, carrots
- Various herbs
- Deviled eggs
- Cheese cubes
- Beach towels
- Bowls of water
- Trays
- Shelled nuts
- Olives

Cooking

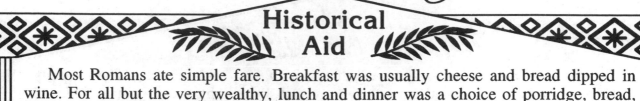

Historical Aid

Most Romans ate simple fare. Breakfast was usually cheese and bread dipped in wine. For all but the very wealthy, lunch and dinner was a choice of porridge, bread, beans or lentils and some fruit or olives.

No one ate pasta because it hadn't been invented yet! There were no tomatoes or potatoes on the menu either. The ancestor of the pizza was made of a paste of chickpeas topped with herbs as imported wheat was expensive.

The food was highly spiced, often with a salty flavoring made of fish insides! Honey was the only sweetener available and Roman shoppers often stopped to buy honey cakes from the bakery shops.

Project

Try some Roman recipes that can be prepared in the classroom.

Directions

1. Divide students into several small work stations to prepare some of the recipes provided.

2. Ingredients that require chopping or slicing, do so before cooking and place in bowls to be measured out by students.

Materials

- Ladle
- Pizza pan or cookie sheet
- Forks, plates and cups
- Napkins
- Ingredients for selected recipes
- Strainer
- Potato masher
- Spatula
- Stove or microwave
- Oven
- Toaster
- Large bowls
- Cheese grater
- Cutting board
- Knives
- Plates
- Spoons
- Large pot
- Electric skillet

CELERY SALAD

1 bunch celery, about eight to ten ribs

3 tablespoons (44 ml) olive oil

2-3 ounces hard cheese such as Parmesan or Romano (about ⅓ cup [79 ml] grated)

1 tablespoon (14.8 ml) lemon juice

Directions:

Grate cheese on largest holes. Clean celery and slice as thin as possible. Toss together all ingredients and serve. Makes about three cups (710 ml).

Roman Recipes

CRUSTULUM (GARLIC BREAD)

Italian bread

1 garlic clove for each student

Olive oil—extra virgin is best

Directions:

Give each student a garlic clove to peel. Meanwhile, slice bread and toast in a toaster. Have each student rub their toast with the peeled garlic on both sides until the garlic is all rubbed in. Drizzle with a little olive oil and eat.

SPICED HONEY GRAPE JUICE

4 cups (946 ml) unsweetened grape juice (Romans would have used wine)

2 cups (473 ml) water

½ cup (118 ml) honey

2 cinnamon sticks

6 tablespoons (89 ml) lemon juice

Directions:

Bring all ingredients to a boil and simmer for ten minutes. Serve warm. Makes eighteen ⅓ cup (79 ml) servings.

CECINA (PIZZA'S ANCESTOR)

2 cans chickpeas (ceci or garbanzo beans)

½ teaspoon (2.45 ml) salt

4 tablespoons (59 ml) olive oil—divided

Dried or fresh basil leaves

Directions:

Drain beans, reserving the liquid. Place beans in a large bowl. Mash beans into a paste with a potato masher, adding about 8 to10 tablespoons reserved liquid to make a smooth paste. Stir in two tablespoons olive oil. Oil a pizza pan or cookie sheet with one tablespoon oil. Spread the batter out onto the oiled pan, patting into a 12" circle. Drizzle remaining oil on top and sprinkle with basil. Bake at 375˚ for 40 to 45 minutes, until light brown. Cecina will not resemble modern pizza! Cut into tiny squares and serve with a spatula. Makes about 30 small squares.

ROMAN BEANS (LIMA BEANS & LETTUCE)

1 tablespoon (14.8 ml) olive oil

1 minced garlic clove

10 ounces frozen baby lima beans, defrosted

3 ribs celery, thinly sliced

1 medium onion, chopped

½ cup (118 ml) chicken broth

½ head iceberg lettuce, cut in big chunks

Directions:

Heat oil in electric skillet. Sauté garlic, celery and onion until onion is tender, about 10 minutes. Add beans and broth, cover. Simmer until beans are tender, about 10 minutes, adding more broth if necessary. Add lettuce and heat, covered, for two minutes. Add pepper to taste if desired. Makes fourteen ¼ cup (59 ml) servings.

Literature

Historical Aid

The Augustin Age, which lasted for about 200 years, was the Golden Age of Roman Literature. Such famous writers as Horace, Ovid, Livy and Virgil lived and wrote during this time.

One of the world's greatest poems of heroic adventure was composed by the most famous Roman poet, Virgil. This twelve-book epic is called the *Aeneid*. It tells the story of the hero Aeneas after the Trojan War. His adventures include a shipwreck and a trip to the underworld, where he learns about his future descendants—the Romans. The books are full of exciting battles, gods and goddesses, jealous suitors and near escapes.

Project

Write an adventure poem and copy it onto a scroll.

Materials

- White butcher paper
- One paper towel roll per scroll
- Tape
- Yarn

Directions

1. Have the students write a poem about a heroic feat or an adventurous escapade.

2. Cut butcher paper into 12 X 18 inch (31 X 46 cm) lengths.

3. Instruct the students to copy their poem onto the butcher paper.

4. Tape the top of the paper to the paper towel roll. Roll up the scroll and tie closed with yarn.

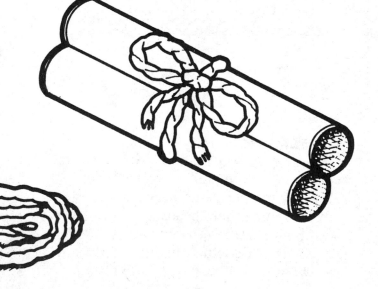

Writing

Routine notes were written on a wax tablet called a *cera* (meaning wax). Beeswax was melted and poured into shallow cavities in wooden tablets. A pointed instrument called a *stylus* was used to write on the wax. The wax could be smoothed and written on again and again. These tablets were hinged so they could be closed to protect the writing.

Roman scribes often used pens dipped in ink made of soot, pitch and octopus ink. They wrote on papyrus, wood or vellum. Vellum was made of thin sheets of animal skin and was very durable. Only the finest books were written on vellum.

Project

Make a wax tablet and practice writing the Roman alphabet.

Materials

- Waxed paper
- Black or dark brown construction paper
- Very sharp pencil
- Clear tape

Directions

1. Cut a piece of waxed paper 20" long. Fold in half lengthwise and again widthwise.

2. Tape to a piece of construction paper.

3. Using a very sharp pencil, practice writing the letters in the Roman alphabet, shown in the box at right. Notice there are only twenty-three letters.

The Roman Alphabet

A B C D
E F G H
I K L M
N O P Q
R S T V
X Y Z

Language

Historical Aid

Latin was the language spoken by the earliest inhabitants of Rome called *Latins*. Even though many conquered peoples continued to speak their own language, Latin became the official language of the Roman Empire.

Latin is the basis of French, Spanish and other Romance languages. Many languages spoken today still contain numerous Latin words.

Project

Learn about the Latin language by playing a word matching game.

Materials

- Word Match-Up page, following
- Pencils

Directions

1. Reproduce one copy of the Word Match-Up page for each student.

2. See how many Latin words they can correctly match.

3. The answers are conveniently located in the box at left.

Answers to Word Match-Up

2	familia
17	villa
28	magnitudo
5	ferox
6	tabula
15	solus
19	lector
9	equus
14	refrigero
11	mimus
26	triplex
13	camelopardalis
23	similis
3	secundus
8	infans
30	matrimonium
25	remotus
20	femina
10	textum
7	medicus
21	infinitas
29	contrarius
16	villanus
1	actor
24	animal
22	clamo
18	pax
27	vigil
12	aqua
4	libertas

Latin Match-Up

Match-up the words by putting the number of the English word in the blank before the correct Latin word.

1. actor	_____ familia
2. family	_____ villa
3. second	_____ magnitudo
4. freedom	_____ ferox
5. fierce	_____ tabula
6. tablet	_____ solus
7. doctor	_____ lector
8. baby	_____ equus
9. horse	_____ refrigero
10. fabric	_____ mimus
11. mime	_____ triplex
12. water	_____ camelopardalis
13. giraffe	_____ similis
14. to cool	_____ secundus
15. alone	_____ infans
16. farmhand	_____ matrimonium
17. country house	_____ remotus
18. peace	_____ femina
19. reader	_____ textum
20. female	_____ medicus
21. endlessness	_____ infinitas
22. acclaim	_____ contrarius
23. alike	_____ villanus
24. creature	_____ actor
25. distant	_____ animal
26. triple	_____ clamo
27. watchman	_____ pax
28. greatness	_____ vigil
29. reverse	_____ aqua
30. marriage	_____ libertas

 © EDUPRESS

Theater

In Rome, serious drama was far less popular than comedy, short farces and pantomime. Tickets were free and the audience was usually loud and unruly. Most comedies included music, singing and ended happily.

The plots often revolved around cases of mistaken identity, and included characters such as cunning slaves, greedy old men and beautiful heiresses. The actors wore comic masks made of stiffened linen painted in an exaggerated style to represent the character's traits. Female characters typically wore white masks.

Project

Make a mask similar to the stiffened linen masks worn by Roman comedy actors.

Materials

- Tempera paint
- Paintbrushes
- String or yarn
- Mixing bowls or dishpans
- Small paper or Styrofoam bowls (one per student)
- Aluminum foil
- Cheese cloth
- Liquid starch
- Newspapers
- Scissors

Directions

1. Cut sheets of foil large enough to cover a student's face. Have the students press the foil over their faces to shape their mask.

2. Cut or tear strips of newspaper. Cut cheesecloth into a piece large enough to cover the foil.

3. Put starch into a bowl or dishpan and dip the strips of newspaper into it.

4. Lay foil form over inverted paper bowl for support. Gently lay pieces of newspaper over foil.

5. Make the final layer with the cheesecloth piece to give the mask a linen-like texture. Allow to dry.

6. Carefully pull foil away from mask. Cut out the eye openings and a large mouth. Poke two holes in the edges and attach yarn or string for ties. Paint with tempera paints.

Sculpture

Roman towns had many sculptures of gods and goddesses, emperors and politicians on display. Families kept sculptures of their ancestors in the home. Buildings and commemorative monuments were adorned with carvings depicting historical events or symbolic stories.

Portrait busts were in such great demand that they were mass produced by art students. Portraiture was important in Roman sculpture. Roman sculptors often combined a Roman portrait head with a copy of a Greek statue of a god.

Project

Make a foil sculpture.

Materials

- Aluminum foil
- Craft sticks
- Clay

Directions

1. Tear off a large sheet of foil.

2. Twist, bend and shape the foil into a pleasing form or try making a person or animal.

3. Poke one end of a craft stick into the sculpture. Anchor the over end in a ball of clay to make it stand up.

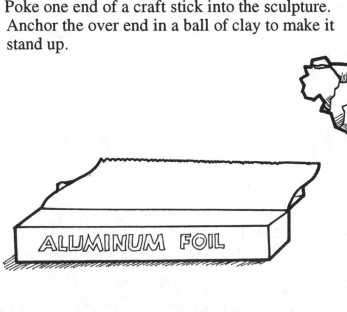

ALUMINUM FOIL

Columns

Historical Aid

Romans erected large single columns as memorials to famous people or events. Sculptors decorated these massive columns with carved horizontal or spiraling bands called *friezes*.

The Emperor, Trajan, built a gigantic column in Rome in 114 A.D. to commemorate a military victory. This column, known as Trajan's Column, stands 150 feet (38 meters) in height. The carved friezes show pictures of battles and army life. The inscription on the bottom shows proportioned lettering. Stonecutters inscribing letters on memorial columns such as Trajan's developed the letter forms we use today.

Project

Build a memorial column to commemorate your school year or events in your community.

Materials

- Butcher paper
- Marking pens
- Scissors
- Tape

Directions

1. Give each student a piece of butcher paper about two feet long.

2. Have the students illustrate each frieze with pictures of what it's like to attend your school or live in your town. Label the pictures in all capital letters. Add serifs or little finishing strokes to the letters as Roman stonecutters did.

3. Roll and tape the pieces to make each section of the column.

4. Display your column in sections or lay it out on the floor to imagine what a Roman memorial column looked like. If possible, affix the column sections to the wall to make it stand up.

Pottery

Historical Aid

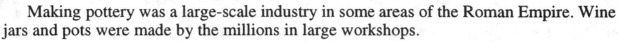

Making pottery was a large-scale industry in some areas of the Roman Empire. Wine jars and pots were made by the millions in large workshops.

Glossy terra cotta pottery called *Samian* ware was very popular throughout the first and second centuries A.D.

Craftsman, typically slaves, made platters, bowls and cups in various sizes. Pottery jars were used to store oil and wine. The jars could be made watertight by sealing them with pitch.

Project

Make a piece of pottery in the Samian style.

Materials

• Red clay

If red clay is not available:
• Flour
• Salt
• Water
• Terra cotta colored acrylic paint
• Bowl
• Waxed paper

Directions

1. To mix clay, combine one cup (236.6 ml) of flour with ½ cup (118.3 ml) salt. Add ⅓ cup (78.87 ml) water, a little at a time. Squeeze the dough with your hands until smooth. Clay is best mixed in small batches.

2. Shape the clay into a pot, bowl, cup or platter. Work on a sheet of waxed paper to keep clay from sticking. Let dry.

3. Paint pottery with terra cotta colored acrylic paint.

Paintings

Historical Aid

The walls in Roman homes and buildings were often decorated with richly colored paintings that made the rooms seem larger and brighter. These wall paintings were usually made with the fresco technique—the paint was applied directly to the wall while the plaster was still damp.

Favorite subjects were garden landscapes, events from Roman mythology and scenes from everyday life.

Roman artists were among the first to develop the skill of drawing in perspective to give their paintings the illusion of depth.

Project

Work as a class to make a mural similar to the wall paintings found in Roman homes.

Directions

1. Tape large pieces of white butcher paper to the walls around the room.

2. Lightly sketch the outlines of the painting. Spread out newspaper to protect the floor.

3. Use bright colors to paint the "walls" just as Roman artists did.

Materials

- White butcher paper
- Pencils
- Masking tape
- Newspapers
- Tempera paint
- Brushes
- Aprons

Mosaics

Historical Aid

Mosaic is an art form in which small pieces of colored glass, brick, pottery or stone are set into mortar to form a picture. These pieces are called *tesserae*. To cover a floor fifty square feet, a craftsman would need fifteen million tesserae!

Mosiacs were used to decorate the floors in homes and public buildings. A particularly impressive display of mosaic floors could be found in the Baths of Caracalla, a public bath in Rome. Public bath houses were common because only the wealthy could afford private bathrooms. The Romans spread mosaic art throughout the Empire.

Project

Make a mosaic.

Directions

1. Draw the outline of a picture or a design on white paper.

2. Cut the colored construction paper into small squares.

3. Spread glue on one small section of the design at a time.

4. Cover the glue with cut paper pieces to fill in the picture.

Materials

- Colored construction paper
- Scissors
- Glue
- Pencil
- White construction paper

Festival

Historical Aid

December 17th was the day the Romans began the festival to honor Saturn, the god of agriculture. This celebration, called *Saturnalia*, lasted from two days to a week! The festival began as a thanksgiving celebration to commemorate the winter planting. It later became a time of merriment when even slaves were given time off to do as they pleased.

People celebrated by feasting, visiting friends and exchanging gifts. The most popular gifts were wax candles and small clay figures.

Project

Make hand-dipped wax candles to exchange with your friends.

Directions

1. Fill electric skillet ½ full with water and begin heating to boiling. Break paraffin into small pieces and fill soup cans ⅔ full. Place cans in water to melt wax.

2. While wax is melting tie a length of thread to the wick of each birthday candle.

3. Carefully remove cans from water. Place on a table protected with newspapers. Have the students dip their candles into the melted wax. Let candles cool between dips by having students slowly count to 30. The more dips, the fatter the candle.

Materials

- Birthday candles
- Paraffin or old candle stumps
- Empty soup cans
- Electric skillet
- Old crayons for color (optional)
- Thread
- Hot pads
- Newspaper

© EDUPRESS

Roman Take-Out

Historical Aid

Romans ate out at fast food restaurants similar to the ones we visit today! These take-out restaurants called *popinas* were popular eating places for ordinary Romans. Customers could take out their food or go inside, past the counter, to eat their meal. Paintings on the wall advertised what was on the menu.

Most of the apartment buildings were made of wood and were serious fire hazards. When an emperor declared that cooking in apartments was illegal, people had to go out to eat or buy take-away food.

Project

Set up a Roman *popina* or take-out restaurant.

Directions

1. Make posters advertising the items for sale. Post on the walls.

2. Start to heat soup in crock pot on high (it will take one hour to heat four cans of soup).

3. Assign students to be set up crew or cooks. Have the set up crew arrange two tables—one serving table and one to be the "counter". Allow cooks to cut bread and fruit into small portions and arrange food on trays or dishes.

4. Let the students take turns being servers and customers, using pennies for Roman coins.

Materials

- Paper
- Olives
- Bread
- Crock pots
- Bowls
- Spoons
- Canned lentil soup
- Marking pens or crayons
- Assorted fruit such as watermelon, grapes, apples
- Grape drink (recipe on page 29)
- Two big tables or desks pushed together
- Trays or serving dishes
- Cups
- Napkins
- Cutting boards
- Knives
- Ladles
- Pennies

Games

Historical Aid

Roman children played games very similar to games still played by children today. Board games similar to checkers and parcheesi were very popular.

Marbles and jacks were other favorites. The jacks of today are very different than those a Roman girl would have played with—hers would have been made with animal bones!

Dice games were played by both children and adults and the dice looked identical to the ones we use today. Other pastimes included playing with leather balls, dolls, wooden hoops and swords and a stick game similar to hockey.

Project

Have a game day to try out the kinds of games enjoyed by Roman children.

Materials

- Parcheesi game
- Checker set
- Jacks
- Marbles
- Chalk

Directions

1. Set up several game stations featuring jacks, marbles, checkers and Parcheesi. Allow the students time to try all of the games. Use the directions on the following page for marbles and jacks.

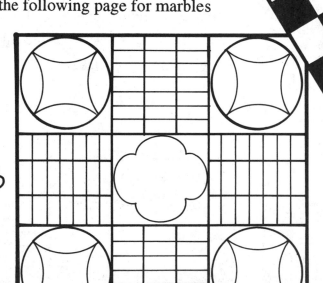

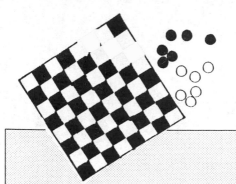

Games

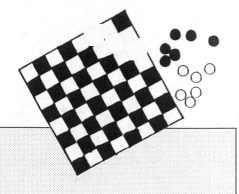

JACKS
Two to Four Players

1. Spread out the jacks.

2. The first player throws the ball up and scoops up one jack. The ball is allowed to bounce one time before it is caught.

3. Player continues scooping up one jack at a time until all jacks are picked up. If the player fails to pick up a jack or fails to catch the ball after one bounce, his turn is over. Play passes to the next person.

4. On the next round of play, each player who succeeded in the first round will pick up the jacks two at a time. Those who failed will retry with ones. Each successive round will add one to the number of jacks to be picked up at one time.

5. The game is won by the first player to successfully pick up all of the jacks on one throw.

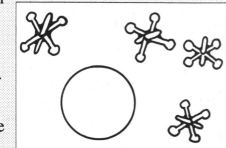

MARBLES
Two to Four Players

1. Using chalk, draw a circle about two feet across on the playground. Place several small marbles in the circle, arranging them into a cross.

2. The first player balances a large marble (a shooter) between his thumb and index finger. Keeping one knuckle on the ground, he flicks the marble toward a marble in the circle. The object is to knock at least one marble out of the circle while keeping the shooter in the circle. If successful, the player continues to shoot from wherever the shooter comes to rest.

3. A turn ends when a player fails to knock out a marble or his shooter leaves the circle. Keep score of how many marbles are knocked out of the circle.

4. Arrange the marbles back into a cross for the next player. The player who has knocked out the most marbles at the end of play is the winner.

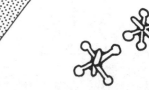

Crowns

Historical Aid

In ancient Rome, the highest honor given to a victorious general was a parade through the capital called a *triumph*. The general wore a crown of laurel and rode in a procession that included trumpeteers, prisoners, senators, family members and soldiers with their booty.

Over the years, it became a law that only emperors could receive a triumph. In addition to a laurel crown, a slave would stand holding a golden crown over the emperor's head as the people cheered. From the reign of Constantine, the crown was regarded as the symbol of royal power. Later, European rulers borrowed the practice of wearing a crown from the Romans.

Project

Make a set of crowns like the ones worn by a Roman Emperor during his triumph.

Materials

- Tagboard
- Green construction paper
- Aluminum foil
- Toothpicks
- Gold spray-paint
- Scissors
- Glue
- Stapler

Directions

1. To make a laurel leaf crown, cut leaf shapes from green construction paper. Glue to a narrow strip of tagboard long enough to circle the student's head. Staple into a circle to form a crown.

2. To make a gold crown, cut a crown shape from tagboard (Roman crowns were often very narrow). Cover with foil. Using a toothpick, lightly trace designs to make the crown appear embossed. Spray-paint gold. Staple into a circle to form a crown.

 © EDUPRESS

Soldiers

Historical Aid

Soldiers were important men in the Roman period, during peace time as well as in battle. During times of peace, the soldiers built roads, bridges, tunnels, walls and aqueducts. No one doubts that Rome owed her great empire to these highly trained, well-armed legions of men.

Soldiers had to be tough. Their packs and armor weighed nearly 90 pounds (40 kg) and they hiked up to 20 miles (30 km) a day! They hauled their own food, water, dishes and tools in their packs.

Project

Make a supply list for a Roman soldier.

Materials

- Paper
- Pencil
- Bathroom scale
- Books

Directions

1. Have the students make a list of what they would need to pack if they were planning a backpacking trip through Europe that would last two years.

2. Visualize the weight of 90 pounds of pack and armor by stacking books on a bathroom scale. Have the students imagine hiking 20 miles carrying all those books!

Gladiators

Historical Aid

Gladiators were not soldiers, but trained warriors who fought battles for entertainment. Most gladiators were slaves or criminals. It was possible for a gladiator to win his freedom if he were able to survive fierce battles in the arena.

Some gladiators wore visored helmets and carried shields. However, this armor was for decoration and did not offer much protection. A *Thracian* is a gladiator that carried a small shield and fought with a curved dagger. Thracian's shields were small and decorative. Other weapons included various nets, swords and spears.

The fight would usually continue until one man was killed. There is evidence that there were even some female gladiators.

Project

Make a small shield.

Materials

- Cardboard
- Aluminum foil
- White glue
- Liquid black shoe polish
- Newspapers
- Paper towels
- Sponge

Directions

1. Cut a circle with an 11 inch (28 cm) diameter out of cardboard.

2. Make a design on tagboard with a **thick** stream of glue. Dry overnight or until glue has hardened completely.

3. Make a mixture of equal parts glue and water. Paint over the entire surface of the shield.

4. Tear off a piece of foil about 13 inches (33 cm) long. Crumple the foil lightly, then uncrumple and press over the glued surface. Begin in the center and work out.

5. Use a sponge to apply shoe polish over the surface of the shield. Wipe gently with paper towel to highlight the raised areas. Let dry.

6. Tape or glue a tagboard handle to the back of the shield. Gladiators wore this type of shield on their forearm, so make the handle big enough to slip on the arm.

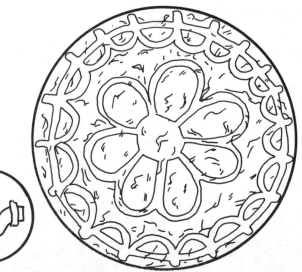

Chariot Races

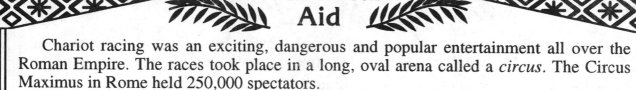

Historical Aid

Chariot racing was an exciting, dangerous and popular entertainment all over the Roman Empire. The races took place in a long, oval arena called a *circus*. The Circus Maximus in Rome held 250,000 spectators.

The chariot itself consisted of a two-wheeled cart drawn by as many as four powerful, fast horses. The chariot bed was a platform with an open back that only held one or two passengers. At the signal the charioteers, dressed in their team's color, raced around the *spina* or central barrier of the arena. Skilled charioteers became heroes if they survived.

Project

Have a mock chariot race.

Materials

- Cardboard boxes
- Traffic cones or similar markers
- Masking tape
- Scissors or knife
- Blue, red, white and green construction paper
- Gold foil-covered chocolate coins (optional)

Directions

1. Cut out the bottom of a cardboard box. Cut out handles on sides of box and reinforce with tape.

2. Mark starting line with tape (or chalk). Place cones in a line to make spina or barrier around which the "chariots" race.

3. Divide students into teams—Reds, Blues, Greens and Whites. These were actual Roman team names. Pin a piece of paper to the student's shirts to identify team color.

4. Race in heats of four (1 member of each team). Race around the course seven times counterclockwise, just like the Roman charioteers in the Circus Maximus.

5. Keep score: 4 points for first, 3 points for second, 2 points for third and 1 point for last place.

6. Reward the victors with a palm branch cut from green construction paper and some gold coins.

Athletic Games

Historical Aid

At one time, Romans enjoyed so many holidays that the emperor had to limit them to 135 days a year. Most holidays were religious festivals in honor of gods and goddesses.

Wealthy Romans would sponsor free public entertainments in outdoor arenas called amphitheaters. The most famous amphitheater in Rome was the Coliseum. It was large enough to seat 50,000 spectators.

Athletic games were popular entertainments at festivals. These games might include foot races and sprints, the long jump, javelin and discus throws, as well as wrestling, boxing and chariot races.

Project

Plan a day for students to compete in ancient, yet familiar, athletic games.

Materials

- Frisbees
- Tape measures
- Chalk to mark start lines
- Masking tape

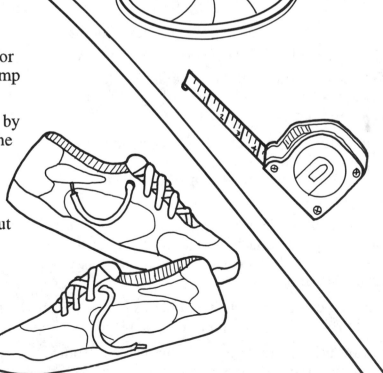

Directions

1. Set up four game stations. Measure 200 yards (180 meters) for a foot race. Measure 50 feet for the sprints. Mark a starting line for the long jump and the frisbee throw.

2. Students can mark the finish lines for the races by stretching out a long piece of masking tape. The first runner to break through the tape is the winner.

3. Divide students into four groups. Rotate the athletes through all four stations allowing about 15-20 minutes per station.